IT CAME FROM THE FAR SIDE

IT CAME FROM
THE FAR SIDE

by Gary Larson

WARNER BOOKS

IT CAME FROM
THE FAR SIDE

"Well, if you're almost ready,
I'm dressed to kill."

Belly button slipknots

5

"Randy's goin' down!"

Late at night, his own stomach would
foil Gordon's attempt at dieting.

"Well, I guess I'll have the ham and eggs."

In the days before soap

"Oh, look, Roger! Nerds! ... And some little nerdlings!"

"Good heavens—just *look* at you! You've been down at the Fergusons' porch light, haven't you?"

"Hold up, Niles. It says here, 'These little fish have been known to skeletonize a cow in less than two minutes.' ... Now *there's* a vivid thought."

9

Thwarting the vampcow

"Eddie! I've told you a hundred times never to run with that through the house!"

"Well, shoot. I just can't figure it out.
I'm movin' over 500 doughnuts a day,
but I'm still just barely squeakin' by."

"Well, I'm not sure. ... You
don't carry any other styles?"

11

In his heart, Willy knew the
ants were being very foolish.

12

Mitch loses a dollar.

"Oh, that's so disgusting—I guess a fly strip and you in the same house just aren't going to work out."

13

"C'mon, Gordy. ... Are you *really* choking, or just turning green?"

Randy and Mark were beginning to sense the wolves were up to no good.

14

"Rise and shine, everyone! ... It's a beautiful day and we're all going to the window sill."

"Oooo! Oooo! ... Are you a good witch or a bad witch?"

Childhood innocence

Tarzan visits his childhood home.

16

Where the buffalo cruise

17

When a tree falls in the forest and no one is around.

Pirate school

"Looks like the bank's been hit again.
Well, no hurry—we'll take the big horse."

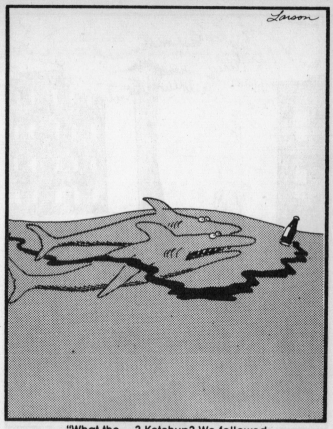

"What the —? Ketchup? We followed
a *ketchup* trail for three miles?"

19

Between classes at the College
of Laboratory Assistants

"Barrow"—precursor to the game
of "wheelbarrow"

"To the death, Carlson! Hang on to the death!"

The rhino in repose

21

"Look out, Thak! It's a ... a ... dang!
Never can pronounce those things!"

Channel 42—your vampire station

"Mr. Bailey? There's a gentleman here who claims an ancestor of yours once defiled his crypt, and now you're the last remaining Bailey and ... oh, something about a curse. Should I send him in?"

Life on cloud eight

"Mom! He's doing it again!"

"Be back by suppertime, Hump ...
and, as always, you be careful."

HAMSTERETTES..............3⁹⁵
THE THUMPER SPECIAL...........5⁹⁵

NORWAY RATS
  Small...................2⁵⁰
  Med....................3²⁵
  Jumbo..................5⁹⁵

PYTHON'S PLATE.............8⁹⁵
(The works)

Down at the Eat and Slither

"Are you serious? Look at our arms! If anything, I'm *twice* as tan as you are."

"Don't ask me how it happened, Stan ... just get your abdomen over here and get me unstuck!"

Still in its early stages, the Olduvai
Pothole claims its first victim.

Punk porcupines

The shark on the go

"Hey! I'm coming, I'm coming—just cross your legs and wait!"

"We'll ask you one more time, stranger—if you're *really* a cowboy from the Rio Grande, then why ain't your legs bowed or your cheeks tan?"

29

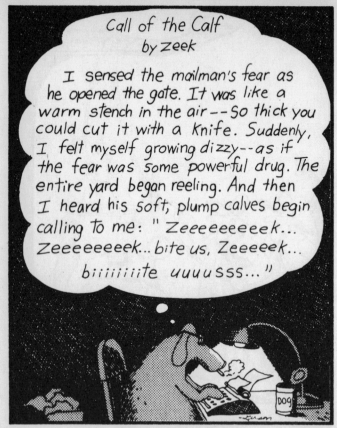

Creative dog writing

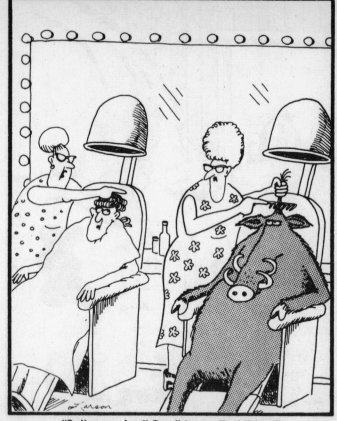

"Betty, you fool! Don't tease that thing!"

30

"Is it still there?"

"Varmints! ... You're all just a bunch of cheatin' varmints!"

And then Jake saw something
that grabbed his attention.

"Oh, what a cute little Siamese. ... Is he friendly?"

Igor goes shopping.

"Python ... and he's home."

When worlds collide

Knowing how it could change the lives of canines everywhere, the dog scientists struggled diligently to understand the Doorknob Principle.

"Matthews ... we're getting another one of those strange 'aw blah es span yol' sounds."

35

The Arnolds feign death until the Wagners, sensing
the sudden awkwardness, are compelled to leave.

"And *now* here comes Zubulu. If
this isn't weird—middle of the night,
and for some reason we're all restless."

"A cat killer? Is that the face of a cat killer?
Cat *chaser* maybe. But hey—who isn't?"

37

After reaching the far side, Tonga cut the bridge—
sending the outraged suburbanites into the river
below. Their idol was now his ... as well as its curse.

Billy leaves home to join the zoo, but returns
the next day after being told that, as an
animal, he was just "too common."

"Sidney! I made a mistake! ... Deposit the $50 *check* into savings, and put the $500 in *cash* into checking!"

Through patience and training, Professor Carmichael believed he was one of the few scientists who could freely visit the Wakendas.

The bride, best man, and ushers of Frankenstein

Forest violence

40

"I just can't tell from here. ... That could either be our flock, another flock, or just a bunch of little m's"

While the city slept, Dogzilla moved quietly from building to building.

"This was *your* suggestion, Edna! ... 'Let's
play Twister, everyone, let's play Twister!'"

Hannibal's first attempt

42

"Notice all the computations, theoretical scribblings, and lab equipment, Norm. ... Yes, curiosity killed these cats."

Luposlipaphobia: The fear of being pursued by timber wolves around a kitchen table while wearing socks on a newly waxed floor.

43

"Wait a minute, Stan. ... These are good hubcaps. If we don't take 'em, it's a cinch some other bears will."

Duggy's science project gets in Mr. Og's hair.

Nanoonga froze—worrying less about ruining a good head than he did the social faux pas.

When fleas go unchecked

46

Tarzan contemplates another entry.

"If there're monsters moving in next door, Danny, you just ignore them. The more you believe in them, the more they'll try to get you."

47

Suddenly, everything froze. Only the buzzing of the tsetse flies could be heard. The crackling grass wasn't Cummings returning to camp after all, but an animal who didn't like to be surprised.

The nightmare makers

The Great Nerd Drive of '76

"Puuuuut the caaaaat ouuuuuuuuut ... Puuuuut
the caaaaat ouuuuuuut ..."

Stupid clerks

"The picture's pretty bleak, gentlemen. ... The world's climates are changing, the mammals are taking over, and we all have a brain about the size of a walnut."

Tempers flare when Professors Carlson and Lazzell, working independently, ironically set their time machines to identical coordinates.

The morning dew sparkled on Bill's web. The decoys were in place, his fly call was poised, and luck was in the air.

At Maneaters Anonymous

Garbage dumps of the wild

"Saaaaaay, aren't you a stranger in these parts? Well, I don't *take* candy from *strangers*."

"Well, we just took the wrong exit. I know this breed, Morrison—you have to watch them every minute or wham, they'll turn on you."

The livestock would gather every morning, hoping for one of Farmer Dan's popular "airplane" rides.

"Whoa! This just looks like regular spaghetti! ... Where's my Earthworms Alfredo?"

"C'mon, c'mon! You've done this a hundred times, Uzula;
the vines *always* snap you back just before you hit. ...
Remember, that's *National Geographic* down there."

In God's kitchen

The fords of Norway

"Now, I want you all to know this cat's *not* from the market—Rusty caught it himself."

"The big fellah's gonna be A-OK, Mrs. Dickerson. Now, a *square* knot would've been bad news, but this just appears to be a 'granny.'"

58

"Sorry to intrude, ma'am, but we thought we'd come in and just sort of roam around for a few minutes."

"C'mon, Arlene. Just a few feet in and then we can stand."

A lucky night for Goldy

Invertebrate practical jokes

"Open the gate! It's a big weiner dog!"

"I've seen this sort of thing before, Baxter ... and it's *not* a pretty sight."

As Harriet turned the page, a scream escaped her lips: There was Donald—his strange disappearance no longer a mystery.

62

Testing whether or not animals "kiss"

"Oh, yeah? If you're alone, then whose eye is *that*?"

As quickly as it had started, the egg fight was over.

Early business failures

64

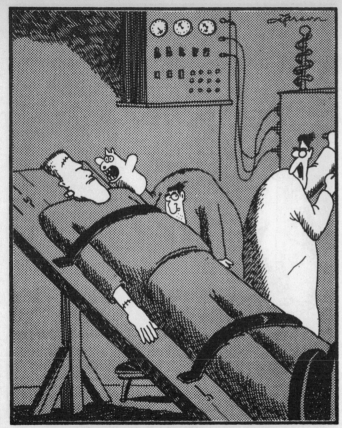

"Igor! Get that Wolfman doll out of his face! ...
Boy, sometimes you really are bizarre."

"Hey! I can hear the traffic!"

Shark nerds always ran the projector.

When careers and allergies collide

"Rusty! Two points!"

Animal game shows

"You're gonna be OK, mister, but I can't say
the same for your little buddy over there. ... The
way I hear it, he's the one that mouthed off
to them gunfighters in the first place."

"Never mind the name. You just tell your boss some *thing* is here to see him!"

Butterflies from the wrong side of the meadow

71

"Yup. This year they're comin' along reeeeeeal good. ... Course, you can always lose a few to an early frost or young pups."

"And the next thing I knew, the whole ship just sunk right out from under me. So what's the deal with you? ... You been here long or what?"

When snakes try to chew gum and crawl at the same time

And then, he slooooooowly lifted the bucket of lard to his lips, and with a low, guttural sound, began to drink!

Gross stories

"Hey, look. No. 1, we're closed, No. 2, I
only work here, and No. 3, we don't
like your kind in here anyway."

"Check this guy out, Lois. ... Artificial for sure."

74

Whenever geese pass through tunnels

"So what's this? I asked for a *hammer!* A hammer!
This is a crescent wrench! ... Well, maybe it's
a hammer. ... Damn these stone tools."

Hit elephants

The 100-meter mosey

Working alone, Professor Dawson stumbles into a bad section of the petri dish.

At the rubber man factory

"Don't be 'fraid, Dug. Me teach him sit on finger. ... Closer, Dug, closer."

"You have to prime it, you know."

Practical jokes of the wild

Edgar finds his purpose.

"He's using blanks—pass it on."

"Oo, Sylvia! You've got to see this! ...
Ginger's bringing Bobby home, and even
though her jaws can crush soup bones, Bobby
only gets a few nicks and scratches."

"Once in a while couldn't we
just have some pasta?"

"For crying out loud, Doris. ... You gotta drag that
thing out *every* time we all get together?"

"You know those teeny tiny little birds that walk around so trustingly inside a crocodile's mouth? Well, I just been eatin' those little guys like popcorn."

Saturday morning in the Garden

82

Across town in the snake district

"Mom! Theron's dried his bed again."

"Listen. You want to be extinct? You want them to shoot and trap us into oblivion? ... *We're* supposed to be the animals, so let's get back out there and *act* like it!"

"Louise! C'mon over here. ... I think we got some bug spreadin' through the store."

Eventually, Stevie looked up: His mother was nowhere in sight, and this was certainly no longer the toy department.

"Looks like another one of those stupid
'Incredible Journey' things."

"You know, Bjorg, there's something about holding
a good, solid mace in your hand—you just look
for an excuse to smash something."

The invaluable lizard setter

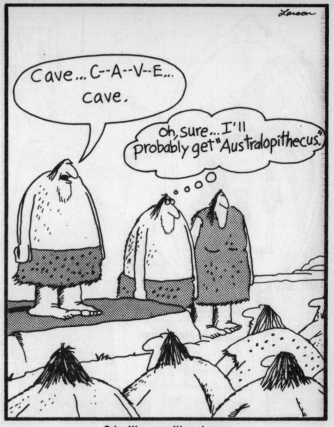

Primitive spelling bees

The heartbreak of remoras

Testing the carnivore-proof vest

88

Single-cell sitcoms

"Mom! Allen's makin' his milk foam!"

At the Comedians' Cemetery

"Now watch this. He'll keep that chicken right there until I say OK. ... You wanna say OK, Ernie?"

"*That's* him! *That's* the one! ... I'd recognize that silly little hat *any*where!"

"Hold still, Omar. ... Now look up. Yep. You've got something in your eye, all right—could be sand."

Seymour Frishberg: Accountant of the Wild Frontier

Cattle hustler

"Sure, I'll draw, mister—but first you gotta say the magic word. ... Didn't your mother ever teach you the magic word?"

Canine social blunders

"According to the map, this should be the place—but it sure don't look right to me. ... Well, we're supposed to die around here *somewhere*."

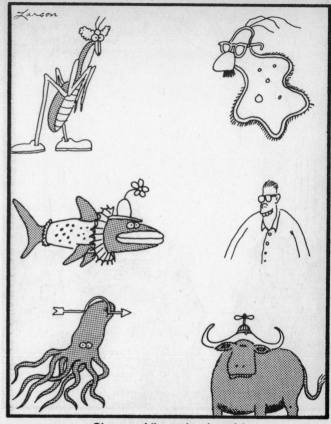

Clowns of the animal world

"Hors d'oeuvre?"

The can of Mace lay where it had fallen
from Bill's hand, and, for a moment,
time froze, as each pondered the
significance of this new development.

When vultures dream

Eventually, the chickens were able to drive a
wedge between Farmer Bob and Lulu.

Interplanetary luggage mix-ups

"C'mon, c'mon—it's either one or the other."

Eventually, Murray took the job—but his friends never did speak to him again.

"Sorry ... we're dead."

Farmer Brown froze in his tracks; the cows
stared wide-eyed back at him. Somewhere,
off in the distance, a dog barked.

"Fuel ... check. Lights ... check. Oil pressure ... check. We've got clearance. OK, Jack—let's get this baby off the ground."

"Well, *I'm* addicted. ... Have you tried Carol's sheep dip?"

Carrots of the evening

Other titles by Gary Larson
To order these or other Warner titles, please see the following
page

Warner Books now offers an exciting range of quality titles by both established and new authors.
All of the books in this series are available from:

Little, Brown and Company (UK) Limited,
P.O. Box 11,
Falmouth,
Cornwall TR10 9EN

Alternatively you may fax your order to the above address. Fax No. 0326 376423.

Payments can be made as follows: cheque, postal order (payable to Little, Brown and Company) or by credit cards, Visa/Access. Do not send cash or currency. UK customers and B.F.P.O. please allow £1.00 for postage and packing for the first book, plus 50p for the second book, plus 30p for each additional book up to a maximum charge of £3.00 (7 books plus).

Overseas customers including Ireland, please allow £2.00 for postage and packing for the first book, plus £1.00 for the second book, plus 50p for each additional book.

NAME (Block Letters) ....

ADDRESS ....

....

☐ I enclose my remittance for _____

☐ I wish to pay by Access/Visa Card

Number ☐☐☐☐☐☐☐☐☐☐☐☐☐☐☐☐

Card Expiry Date ☐☐☐☐